TOYE

समाप्ति की तिथि /Date of Expiry   प्रवेशों की संख्या /No. of Entries

2/12/1999   MULTIPLE

विशेष पृष्ठांकन /Special Endorsement

U.S. IMMIGRATION

GW00838324

2000

OSHOEK
75
A S
2012-05-31
DEPARTURE
PASSPORT CONTROL

SAHAR AIRPORT BOMBAY
VISA
12 AUG 1999
IMMIGRATION - III

BR1371MMBRUIMMBRUIMMBRUIMMBRUIMM
IMMIGRATION
BRUNEI DARUSSALAM
INTERNATIONAL AIRPORT
A9
137
2 8 AUG 1999
VISIT PASS Reg No.
PERMITTED TO ENTER AND REMAIN IN
BRUNEI DARUSSALAM FOR THIRTY
DAYS FOR SOCIAL VISIT ONLY FROM
THE DATE SHOWN ABOVE.

BRUIMMBRUIMM

31 AUG 1999
DEPARTED
INTERNATIONAL AIRPORT

A 209923
REPUBLIC OF INDIA
VISA
TOYE
उपनाम /Surname
भारत गणराज्य

VISA

IMMIGRATION
ARRIVED
29 JAN 2004
BRISBANE AIRPORT
145P
AUSTRALIA

IMMIGRATION
5WB

E-12KGN
27

SWAZILA

£4.99 2011
a

global gypsy

black & white

gerar toye

www.globalgypsy.com

global gypsy - black & white
ISBN 0-9583609-3-6
First edition
2007
Copyright gerar toye

Printed in China

Imagist Publishing
global gypsy gallery
P.O.Box 170
Karamea, West coast
Aotearoa (New Zealand)
nz@globalgypsy.com
oz@globalgypsy.com (Australia)
euro@globalgypsy.com (Europe)
Imagist merchandise of cards, posters, jigsaws and original photographs are available from the web site
www.globalgypsy.com

For anyone who
wants to take the risk
of coming to their senses
and losing their minds
for their souls to evolve

Creating this book was made more pleasurable by Jim Morrison and the Doors for an American prayer and more great music from Laurie Anderson, Pink Floyd, Talking Heads and Van Morrison for Poetic Champions Compose. Richard Bach for Illusions and Paulo Cohelo for his books. Woody Allen, Monty Python and the Simpsons for their humour. Shiva for the charis and herbs which made the sounds better and the imagery flow. Paul Murray the visionary from Karamea for his support. Deirdre for help in Ireland. Manon, Nirav and all the other translators who have offered their time to translate the quotes into the 15 languages so far. Kapil Arn and the other photographic artists whose spontaneity enhance the last section of this book and the thousands of travellers and supporters with whom I shared so much on these twenty years on the road

Terimah Kasih -I receive your love
Namaste- I honour you

I travelled twenty thousand kilometres before I realised the best journey was within. I could not have begun my spiritual journey had it not been for my constant desire to explore my potential. That desire was stronger than the fear of the unknown.

Journal writing was a necessary part of my personal growth. It helped me clarify any confusing feelings & I felt safe enough to express them there. Having grown up with proverbs & quotes from others I found myself reflecting or rejecting what I thought they had to offer. Most of what I was feeling and realising I could not find in books and so started writing my own axioms, which when placed next to one of my photographs in my journal the process was enhanced. The first was "Reality is for those with no imagination".

The quotes are not affirmations, just starting points, where they take us depends on how far we want to go. Their meanings change as we grow and repeatedly investigate the tangent, especially when compared with our latest experiences. The quotes have served my questioning mind. They were all tangents I visited which allowed me to express through words, a plane of existence I felt, an ultimate truth realised. I found that once the experience was summarised & only then could I move on.

I had difficulty believing most things I had been told by others, in books & by the church. I chose not to believe anything unless it resonated with what I felt. I believe we come into this world as wise simple beings, then moulded by family, television, advertising media & society.

Realisation does not mean understanding something new, but recognising something known but long forgotten. Quotes not credited with an author have come from my experiences & I admit wisdom cannot be given only earned. No doubt many people have felt these ideas before.

I wrote "If you want the best view you may have to climb to the top". A friend commented that career devoted people would love the motivation but that is not what I intended. This world is a mess because of financial motivation & greed while I am more interested in spiritual growth and encouraging others to stop & look seriously before they choose a path of materialism.

So I changed the quote to "When you've reached the top, what then?". There are no answers, only questions. None of this book, the images or the insights were planned. It grew through wanting to express what I have felt by listening to my higher self. Its purpose is to inspire others to have the courage to look within, to seek who they truly are, rather than stay caught in the illusion of who they appear to be. It is a book that I would have liked to read early in my life to inspire me to go within rather than to go without.

If you have not explored this world yet then I hope you may be inspired to do so. Go seek your potential. Seek out real experience and the humble simple life. Have no desire for wealth or ego, they are only distractions. Find who you are by creating and allowing the experiences you need to receive the next answer along the way. Follow your heart. Live your passion. Go and live in other cultures. The world is a safe and nuturing space if you believe it, so it is true. The universe will always lead you towards the next opening experience if you are awake and looking for the signs. They have always been there, maybe you didn't give it much thought or even less, have a feeling about it. Travel is the best way to practice intuition as you are not distracted by routine and generally you get to see the outcome of your feelings & decisions instantly.

All the images in this book are spontaneous, capturing moments in life which existed for only fractions of a second. They were taken with old Nikon film cameras with two lenses. I work without a flash or tripod because they restrict spontaneity. Most photographs we see are arranged, posed, manipulated & paid for. Though this type of photography has its uses it is not my way. I thrive on the personal challenge to observe & capture an image unnoticed. Most of my photos are taken from the hip. The risk of missing the shot cannot be compared with the excitement of its possibility. The last section of this book is dedicated to images taken by friends whose spontaniety add value to the quotes.

As a child I was always fascinated by tales that were told by the hitchhikers that Dad would occasionally bring home. Hearing about adventures from afar left me lying awake with a sense of awe and wonderment. The world no longer seemed scary but exciting. We are all born for the journey of Spirit in realising that there is more out there than we can see superficially. Spending two years in Sabah, North Borneo from when I was eight opened up a different world compared to life in Manurewa, South Auckland.

One country that most travellers spoke of was India, people either loved it or hated it. I didn't know why & had to go and experience it for myself. The stories they told were shocking but the way their eyes sparkled when people spoke about it, convinced me to go. India was all they said and much more. On arrival I knew instantly I had lived there previously although, at the time, I had never considered the concept of past lives. I felt so at home there in spirit and have experienced more spiritual culture shock when I would return to the unreality of western society.

India's biggest gift is one of acceptance. Without this practice you risk spontaneous combustion because India pushes all our buttons. The lessons never seem to cease. So much is happening that you cannot drift into the future or past for long before you are jolted back to the present. The amount of growth you can experience in six months in India can be equal to six years in the west. Of course, personal examination and awareness leads to conscious evolution.

Without acceptance, the caste system would never have survived as everyone would want to be of a higher caste which could only cause unhappiness. This is the misery of the western society always wanting twenty percent more than they have. Many people judge the country because of its image rather than considering their own behaviour because they are trapped inside it. Break free and see your life inside out. The absence of crying babies is an incredible sign of acceptance since birth. There is only acceptance or reaction. The choice is yours

Travelling with time restrictions does not allow me to feel the subtle miraculous events of life as I become distracted by the destination instead of being in the present. I find that when I am not seeking a destination or outcome, I start to see the lure of the unknown path and the gifts that are there to be found. Guide books are good for some folk and a good source of bus locations & it's good to know where the other tourists are so you can avoid them.

Many people spend their money going on holiday for a suntan without realising that for the same investment they could wake up and take their soul on holiday. I travelled around the world every year for the price of what most people spent on cigarettes and alcohol.

Travelling alone has allowed me to practice trusting my intuition and to go where I am guided. Sometimes I didn't follow my feelings but dismissed them as illogical and continued in a rational way and life then seem disjointed for a while. When things went wrong It felt like I was delayed or derailed, as if I had missed an opportunity or connection and the flow had stopped. It would take a while for magic to happen again. Descisions come from the mind, whereas choices come from the heart. A choice is never wrong as it engages the universe to provide an experience.

When I allow myself to be guided, miracles come in a never ending stream. So many people refer to miracles as if they were created by some other entity but we create our own when we are grateful for what we have and are in harmony with heart, mind, body and spirit.

Life is the miracle, the universe is conspiring to unfold every opportunity for us to grow. It is ego and mind that sabotage the magic. Now I do not question why miracles happen but rather why they are not happening. It was intuition that saved me from flight UA93 on September 11 as I was offered 2 free tickets if I was to be bumped to the morning flight, an offer I normally planned every year flying through New York

The best adventures I have had are when I have chosen to hitch hike or to travel and eat as locals do. If you stay in luxury hotels and travel in groups you are a tourist. You will have paid to separate yourself from experiencing the culture. Travellers don't know where they are going, whereas tourists don't know where they have been. Travelling alone gives the universe a chance to guide you & feel where you're supposed to be or who you are to meet and the messages that are to be shared. It's the intuitive feeling of being in the right place at the right time, that you've been led to a specific point on the planet with a chance to discover who you really are and why you are here.

We are beings with incredible power. It is no secret! What we imagine, can become reality. When we have a thought, no matter how wonderful, scary or irrational it is, if we hold that thought we create it as a possibility in the universe.

We create ourselves and our world daily and attract every experience whether it be joy, contentment, envy, sorrow, abundance, fear ,love or pain. When we are not creating ourselves anew, in each moment, it is easy to see ourselves as victims which limits our universe and prevents miracles.

Self examination is the continuing practice of discovering who we are. One full moon while tripping in Halong Bay, Vietnam, I realised I am not Gerar Toye but an energy of love which is just hanging out in this skin bag for a while. After all, who am I? Am I not a reflection of you and everyone else who have existed before? Are we not all children of God? Are we not an expression of God herself trying to express who she is, through reaching your potential. We are all alone in this world with everyone else. Alone. All one.

On one of my trips to India I contracted malaria and was given an opportunity to leave this body yet chose to live, after all I had not found the love of my life and now feel that all of my experiences were just a prelude to the adventures my heart would allow. In my twins I found my true love & my teachers. Sickness is a healing and I feel quite honoured to have had the chance to die as it gave me a new perspective on what it is to be truly alive and choose to be here now. It gave me a new sense of gratefulness and passion to love like I've never been hurt and fulfil my dreams. While recovering in hospital in Australia I swore I wasn't going back to India. Like many of the teachings from India they don't seem to become lessons until you have left the country for a while. Within two weeks of leaving hospital I had booked another flight back to India.

Travellers are a special breed of people, one that usually trusts and open up to strangers quickly. They realise that the people in front of them are only going to be there for a short time and don't engage in six months of small talk before they can discuss real issues.

Life as a traveller is a choice made every day and I would rather die fulfilling my dreams rather than experience regret. Eighty percent of people that suffer regret in their lives say it is not from an action but rather from inaction.

If you would like to read more insights of my spiritual journey it is titled 'Catalyst for change" and is on my web site
www.globalgypsy.com

A journey of
a thousand miles,
begins with just one step

Lao Tsu

Reality
is for those
with no
imagination

We cannot discover
new oceans
until we have courage
to lose sight
of the shore

Progress
means
advancing
towards
a more
desirable form

A smile
can neither
be bought
nor sold,
yet is the richest gift
one can give
or receive

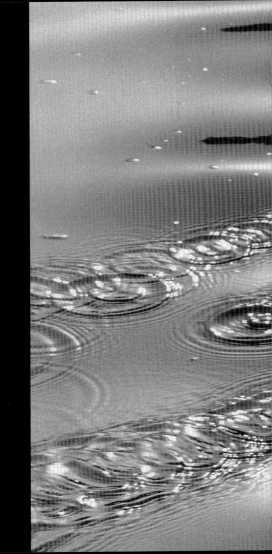

Your actions
will follow
you full
circle round

Indigo Girls

Things
are not as
they seem,
nor are they
otherwise

Does the
chicken
need a
reason?

Seek
and you
will find

Jesus of Nazereth

Limitation
is a creation
of the
mind

I am
what
I am

Popeye the Sailorperson

Travel is fatal to
prejudice,
bigotry and
narrow mindedness

Mark Twain

Your children
will again
be your ancestors

It is good to have
a destination to
journey towards
but it is the
journey
that matters
in the end

Ursula Le Guin

The
difference
between a weed
and a herb is a
judgement

Sure I've smoked, but I never inhaled

Bill Clinton

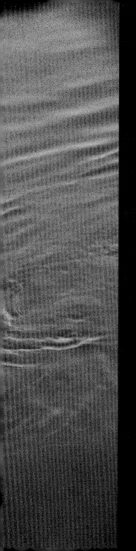

The love of
ourselves is
reflected in our ability to
accept others

Tantra:
love without
a destination

Little is
learned by
speaking

The less
are my needs
the greater is
my home

Reality is
in the eye of
the beholder

Not all who wander are lost

j.r.tolkien

We do not see things as they are,
we see things as
we are

Anaïs Nin

Women,
the hardest
workers on the
planet

When we
look into our
shadows,
we see darkness
is just another
aspect
of the light

You are your own judge,
jailer, worst enemy
and best friend

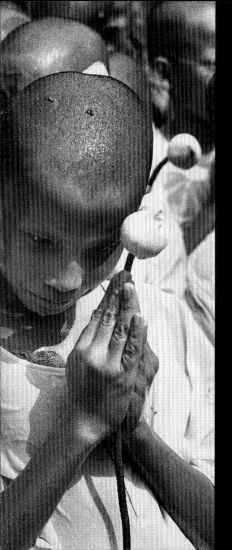

If we don't
go within
we go
without

Neale Donald Walsch

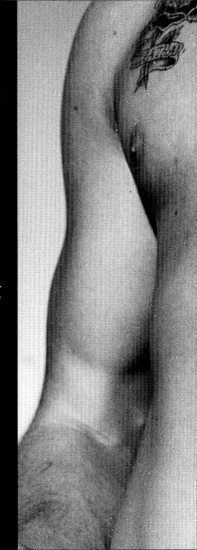

Your past
doesn't have to
restrict your present

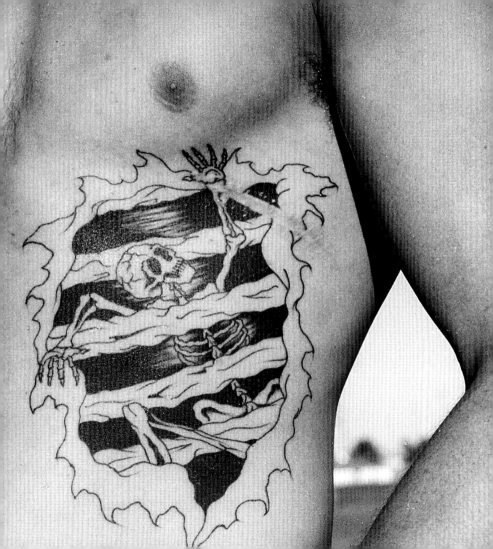

If we could talk
to the animals
the first thing
they would say is
"Please don't eat us"

George Bernard Shaw

The more
you know,
the more
you know
how little
you know

Kill your
television,
before it
kills you

Extinction
is
forever

Obvious

To observe
without judgement
is to witness
the goddess

Whenever two people meet
there is really six present.
here is each man as he sees himself,
each man as he sees the other
and each man how he really is

William James

Shit
Happens

When you say
you're dying
for a smoke,
you're speaking
the truth

Practice random
kindness and
senseless acts
of beauty

Anne Herbert

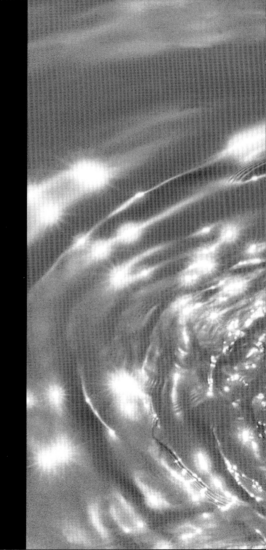

Simple acts
can produce
beauty
and light

We are
all the same,
we just have
different habits

Trust
is the
solution

If you give
someone
a meal
you feed
them
for a day.
Teach them
how to cook
and feed
them for
a lifetime

It's better
to ask
and risk
a no,
than to live
in fear
of rejection

A change
is better
than a holiday

The truth
will set you free,
but it will
piss you off first

If you do what
you've always done,
you'll get what
you've always gotten

If you see someone
without a smile,
give them one of yours

One planet,
twelve million species
to share it

The best way
to have a friend
is to be one

Ralph Waldo Emmerson

Even if you win
the rat race
you're
still a rat

Lily Tomlin

The best feedback
an artist
can receive
is cash

Rarely
do we communicate,
we just take turns talking

When I was young
I knew
everything,
now I'm not so sure

Acceptance
is the art
of letting go

Inside
everyone
lies a
vulnerable
child

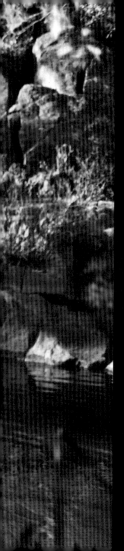

Freedom
is living
each
moment
spontaneously

Hannah Bailly

Control
comes from
ego's fear of
destiny

A hug
is the
perfect gift,
one size fits all
and no
one minds
if you
exchange it

Irving Ball

It's never
too late
to have a
happy
childhood

Tom Robbins

Plates

Page 14: Pilgrimage ,Pashupatinath Temple. Kathmandu, Nepal 1989

Page 16: Outhouse: Ambrose with the Findhorn glass ball on Erraid Island, Iona. West Scotlar 1985.

Page 18: Circumnavigation: Gaff rigged Ketch Lene Marie (1910 Denmark) with 45 knot winds ar a reefed main and missen her 100 tonnes of Oak reached 10 knots, the fastest she had ever bee On a 29 day passage from Yokohama, Japan, to Sitka, Alaska 1987

Page 20: Healing Earth: This strangler fig started with a bird shitting on this Portuguese Hous Look for the profile of a horse behind the left side of the house. Anjuna, Goa, India 1992

Page 22: Smile: Nepal 1989

Page 24: Rowing on the River Ganges. The holy river with 250 000 times more faecal content tha is considered acceptable for a river.

Page 26: Laksmi: When a rupee is placed in your hand and offered to Ganesh the Elephant Go it is received by the trunk and donated to the temple. Ganesh then pats your head as a blessir to remove all your obstacles. Hampi, Karnataka, India 1992.

Page 28: Chicken: Crossing a freshly paved holy cow shit road. This bakes hard in the sun ar reduces dust. Hampi, India, 1992

Page 30: Serendipity: The art of discovery by chance. California, USA

Page 32: Standing Yogi: This Yogi was sitting down, put his ankle behind his head, then stood u Kathmandu, Nepal 1989.

Page 34: Popeye: This man made a bamboo raft so we could raft down a river on the border Myanmar. Golden Triangle, Thailand, 1989

Page 36: Bicycle: Looking down from a bridge across the Ganges, I noticed the space around hi On this day, February the sixth 1989, 16 million people bathed along five kilometres of the river. Th was the biggest gathering in the world's history but was exceeded in 2001 to thirty million.

Page 72: Chillums before lunch in a marquee with hundreds of holy men in Varanasi, India 2001

Page 74: School: Kids without pens write on slates with chalk water and stick and then wash the in the river at the end of the day. Kausani, India 1988

Page 76: KILL YOUR TV: around at a friends house in what is now Manukau city now someor said, "Let's kill the TV". So we did!

Page 78: Stoned Hippos: Glen Rothes. Scotland 1986

Page 80: Goddess Leeda: Orinocco Music Festival, Motueka, Aotearoa, 1994

Page 82: Mirrored Ball. Saw this & just couldn't resist getting bent. 1991 New York USA

Page 84: Bike Sculpture: Berkeley, California, USA 1990

Page 86: Brown snake: The snake was dead someone added the cigarette . Australia, 1983

Page 88: Fatepur Sikri, India

Page 90: Birdman: Hyde Park, London, England 1990

Page 92: Washing: Varanasi, India

Page 94: Water: The hygienic way to drink, Nepal 1989

Page 96: Trust: Bali, Indonesia, 1987

Page 98: Boys in the kitchen: U.P., India. 1987

Page 100: Wanting: Doctor Jack's Free Clinic was being closing early because the monsoons ra had risen to our knees and three bananas were being offered. Calcutta, India, 1995

Page 102: Getting my head shaved, everyone should try it at least once. Gujarat, India 1992

Page 104: Taj Mahal, Agra. This is the dirtiest river I have ever seen. The smell made me vomit.

Page 106: The Truth: Marie , Matthew and Jake. Gypsies of Aotearoa 1999 With an instamatic came I was standing behind Marie and reached around her shoulder to get this spontaneous shot.

142

Page 108: Decisions: Ladakh, Tibetan Plateau. North India 1997

Page 110: High Five. Laughing in the monsoon rain. Old Delhi slum 1998. Shot out the window of a taxi with an instamatic camera

Page 112: Flies: Only seconds after finishing my lemon soda. Colva Beach, Goa, India, 1985

Page 114: Friend: India. Photo by Peter Hemenway ©

Page 116: Cat & rat: Philby was taking pictures of his girlfriend when she saw this happening outside. Nelson, Aotearoa. They both survived. Philby © 1991

Page 118: Artist: This man slows his heart rate and breathing down so he can remain under the footpath for about 20 minutes. Calcutta, India. Mark Glover © 1985

Page 120: Procession of Naga Babas celebrating Shivaratri. Varanasi, India 2001 © gerar toye

Page 122: Birds: Starlings. Aotearoa. Photo by Geoff Moon © 1977

Page 124: Punk: With grandmother, Downtown Sq. Auckland, Aotearoa. Alex Solo © 1982

Page 126: Pilot Whale Stranding: 16 died and 80 were returned to the sea. Due to the slope of the beach, it is physically impossible to gauge with forward sonar and Whales can believe it is open sea. They do not commit suicide, they do not want to burn and die in the sun. Maybe someone can invent a sonar deflector to warn them. Farewell Spit, Golden Bay, Aotearoa. Ross Wearing © 1992

Page 128: Head Hunter: Photo by Kapil Arn ©, Aotearoa

Page 130: Freedom: Last shot on the roll of film. Hand held 1/30th of a second. Kapil Arn © 1972

Page 132: Sheepdog, Australia photo by Kapil Arn

Page 134: Hugs: Te Kohanga Gathering, Aotearoa. Photo by Kapil Arn © 1980

Page 136: Splash: Te Kohanga gathering. Photo by Kapil Arn © 1980

Page 138: Naga Babas in Varanasi for Shiva's birthday. India 2001 © gerar toye

Gerar Toye is a kiwi who roamed the planet for over twenty years. With his unique style of shooting from the hip, he loves playing with spontaneous imagery and especially writing his experiences as axioms to advance the viewers journey

The insights have come from Gerar's journals. Each experience was examined until the tangent was summarised & left to brew.

On reflection the reader is taken to the same starting point. Where it takes you beyond that just requires reflection & imagination.

His life philosophies have been translated into more than fifteen languages.

He is currently raising his twins in Christchurch, script writing and making short films.

Trained as a colour darkroom hand printer and was disillusioned by working with photographers who prostituted the art form. Gerar vowed not to arrange any images or to photograph anything he thought would be commercial. These images were all taken on black & white film with a Nikon F2 and 2 lenses.

Living his dream to travel and be supported as an artist, he spent more than half his life living in the present as he travelled alone, always avoiding winter.

After his first RV in California he converted a 1956 Bedford school bus into his first home. Painted purple he travelled in 'Carpediem' with the gypsies throughout Aotearoa. He also built a house bus in Australia called 'Now.here'

If you have enjoyed this journey another book is planned with the colour images taken from the same journey.

As this work is not found in many outlets on planet earth you may wish to subscribe to the free e-card mailouts which happen occasionally and will let you know of any new creations when they are available.

Limited edition prints and hand printed original photographs are available from the global gypsy gallery in Karamea on the west coast of the south island.

Note cards, jigsaws, posters and sometimes T shirts are available from the web site

If you have any spontaneous images, insights or inspirational stories you would like to share I am always willing to look at your work for future publishing projects.

Up coming projects will be a book of letters submitted by you titled 'What I wish I knew when I was twenty'. See the website for details.

www.globalgypsy.com

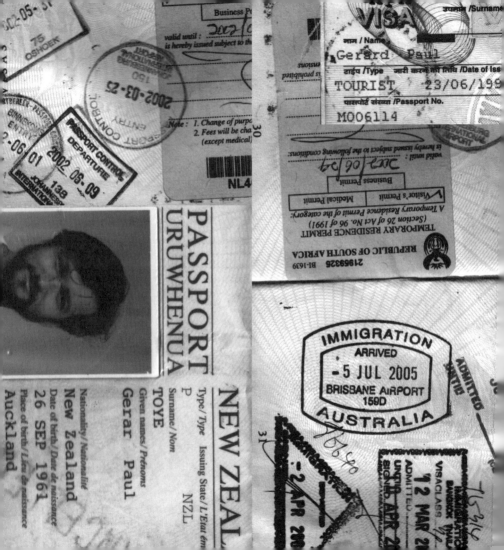